Dominion and Authority
to Rule and Reign

Dominion and Authority to Rule and Reign

by
David T. Demola

Foreword
by Bob Yandian

Unless otherwise indicated, all Scripture
quotations are taken from the *King James Version*
of the Bible.

Dominion and Authority to Rule and Reign
ISBN 0-88144-098-1
Copyright © 1987 by David T. Demola
2177 Oak Tree Road
Edison, New Jersey 08820

Published by CHRISTIAN PUBLISHING SERVICES, INC.
P.O. Box 55388
Tulsa, Oklahoma 74155-1388

Foreword

Knowledge is our greatest weapon God has given against the attacks of the enemy. Isaiah 33:6 says, **. . . wisdom and knowledge shall be the *stability* of thy times . . . .** Stability is what each believer is looking for. It can only come through applying the Word we *know*.

Pastor David Demola has given great insight into our authority as believers. As you read this book, *Dominion and Authority to Rule and Reign*, your knowledge of your position and rights in Christ will increase, as will your stability against Satan's attacks.

Pastor Demola's ministry has blessed the East Coast and is now reaching around the world with crusades in the Caribbean. His church membership has multipied so quickly there is "standing room only" in his auditorium at each of the multiple Sunday services. Hundreds are born again each week and healed by God's power. The fruit of his ministry cannot be denied.

Dave Demola is also my personal friend. He and his wife, Diane, have blessed Loretta and me with their dedication to the Lord and their closeness to us.

It is a privilege to recommend a man and book that will change your life.

Bob Yandian

Prayer

In the name of Jesus, I pray that all those reading this book shall be emptied of anything that may hinder or restrict them from coming into the fullness of what You, Father, desire for them to walk in.

Satan, in the name of Jesus, I command you to stop, right now, your attempts to steal the Word of God out of anybody's heart.

I thank You, Father, that every life is fertile ground for the sowing of the seed of Your Word. I thank You, Father, that we are Your people, and that we have been called to the high calling in an age when sin is rampant, when there is lawlessness all around us. We recognize that the light of Jesus is shining brighter and brighter unto the perfect day, and we rejoice because knowledge, understanding, wisdom and anointing are being given to the Church today in a way like never before. We avail ourselves of these gifts right now. We step into the place of Your power and anointing. We thank You that we are the children of the light, and we walk with the authority of Jesus Christ within us.

We thank You, Father, that we are a chosen generation, a royal priesthood, a holy nation, to deliver forth the praises of Him Who has called us out of darkness into His marvelous light. And in Jesus' name, we will not take a back seat to Satan. We will march as a strong army. We will go forth in the glory of our God, and we will conquer the land, because You have called us to be victorious in You.

Introduction

The key to receiving from God is knowing God! In fact, when you know God, Who HE is, what HE has, and what HE can do, you'll know who YOU are, what YOU have, and what YOU can do. When you know all that, you'll know who Satan is, what he DOESN'T have, and what he CAN'T do.

Our pursuit, therefore, is to know the power of God. To know Who God is, to know the character of God, the heart of God, and the mind of God. You can get to the place where you know what God is going to do next. You can know how God is going to react in certain situations and even know the will of God before you pray.

"How?" you ask. The same way you know somebody in the natural — BY SPENDING TIME WITH GOD.

Part of spending time with God is spending time in His Word. The Word of God reveals the character of God which is what is behind the power of God. God's power is always activated by His Word. When you know the power of God, you'll know that God is unlimited and that He can do more than we ask or even think.

Our Relationship with God

Have you ever met a salesman who was unable to answer all your questions about a product? Did you want to buy what he was selling? The same problem happens among Christians. They try to, in a sense, "sell" Jesus without really knowing "the product."

When you know Who He is, you're able to answer the questions, sharing accurately from your knowledge. Some people get born again, develop a tremendous zeal for God, their heart is filled, but they never take the time to really find out who they are IN CHRIST JESUS. They cannot accurately present Jesus and the Gospel.

Remember, zeal without knowledge is fanaticism. In Romans 10:2 the Apostle Paul points to this problem regarding Israel, . . . **I bear them record that they have a zeal of God, but not according to knowledge.**

Knowledge of God is not only knowing all the power side of God, it is also knowing the side of God that takes into consideration our surrender and determination. It is good to know all about God's power, but we have got to know what it means to be in the fellowship of His suffering. That does not mean we suffer every day for the Lord Jesus with condemnation and doubt. It does acknowledge that there is a price to pay.

You need to come to a point of understanding in your relationship with God when you realize that it is worth everything to serve the Lord Jesus Christ.

There is much authority in understanding. All you need to do is read the first several chapters of the book of Proverbs to find that out. Instruction was given to

Solomon in Proverbs 4:7, **Wisdom is the principal thing; therefore get wisdom: and with all thy getting get understanding.** This principle still applies today. It is in WISDOM and UNDERSTANDING that we learn how to release the supernatural power of God.

Knowledge is the accumulation of facts; wisdom is the application of these facts. You can "accumulate" the scripture and gain tremendous knowledge of it, yet not walk in the fullness of God. This occurs when you don't extract the wisdom of the Word of God through the inspiration of the Holy Ghost. YOUR HEART MUST REACH OUT TO GOD to be able to understand what you read. That is the difference between accumulating facts and applying the facts with wisdom into the situations of your life.

When you read the Word of God by direction of the Holy Spirit, seeking the understanding and knowledge of Who Jesus really is, the Holy Spirit can begin to unveil and reveal Jesus to you. That's when you gain illumination or revelation knowledge. It comes forth by the Spirit of God. The Holy Spirit is the author of the scripture, and it was He Who inspired holy men of God as they spoke and wrote. The Greek word translated *inspired* in English literally means "God breathed."

You can't pick up the Bible and expect to study it as a historical book. You must study it under the same inspiration with which it was written. As Jesus said in John 14:26:

> **But the Comforter, which is the Holy Ghost, whom the Father will send in my name, he shall teach you all things, and bring all things to your remembrance, whatsoever I have said unto you.**

The Holy Spirit will unveil and clear up what you have already been taught through the scripture. The Holy Spirit cannot reveal what you have no knowledge of. Therefore, you need to read the Bible for the understanding, and NOT in a literary sense. Studying the Word of God has to be done consistently in order to extract the truth behind it and enable you to share from knowledge.

A Man After God's Heart

Every time God lifted up the curtain of revelation to a man in the Bible, the first thing revealed to him was God's original plan for man. God lifted up the curtain of revelation to a prophet named David (notice that David was not only a shepherd boy and a king, according to Acts 2:30 he was also a prophet). In Psalm 8:4,5 David asks of God:

> **What is man, that thou art mindful of him? and the son of man, that thou visitest him?**
>
> **For thou hast made him a little lower than the angels, and hast crowned him with glory and honour.**

The word **angels** here is translated from the Hebrew root word *eloihym*, meaning "gods," or "God." This verse then should read: "Thou hast made him a little lower than God [Deity] Himself." Keep in mind that glory and honor are NOT sickness and poverty. In the sixth verse of this psalm, David goes on to state, **Thou madest him to have dominion over the works of thy hands; thou hast put all things under his feet.**

David, a student of the Word of God, reflected through the pages of Genesis and saw Adam and Eve's position in the garden. They were given authority, power and dominion over the works of God's hand, yet they "blew it." David also had a problem understanding who man really is because of his own lifestyle — and God was showing him.

Some of us, because of our lifestyles and the things that we go through in life, lose our position of authority in God. We don't understand that God doesn't bless us *because* of us, He blesses us *in spite* of us.

Each time you have a problem understanding God, He just lifts up the curtain of revelation. He begins to show you who you really are in the light of who He said you are: according to how He made you to be (not in the light of what you were told you were). As with David, God does not look on the outward appearance; God looks on the heart. (Review 1 Sam. 16:1-12, especially verse 7.)

Sin hinders you from receiving from God. Don't think God condones sin, as in the case of David, who failed miserably after being chosen by God. It was because David knew how to REPENT OF HIS SIN that God could speak to him in spite of the flaws in his life. It was because he had a heart after God, because of his sincerity with God, because his heart was pure before God.

If there was ever a man who ran away, if there was ever a man who feared and complained, if there was ever a man who hid and questioned God — David was that man. Yet his triumphs and victories, by the grace of God, prove that God looks far beyond appearances.

Just looking at how God opened up David's spiritual understanding to be able to see into this tremendous realm of spiritual authority which God established in the Garden of Eden is further proof of how God can turn a life around and unveil His plan and will to that person. David's understanding of this tremendous area of dominion and authority is still hidden from some scholarly people today who refuse to submit to God's plan and not man's. WHAT A TRAGEDY!

The Reality of the Word

For many years, one of the major problems that the Church has had is its attitude of "holding on until the end," of making it to heaven with only rags and having God exchange the rags in heaven for a crown. Because of this attitude, Christians have been whipped, beaten and kicked by the devil.

The first thing about you that has to be changed is your attitude toward yourself! You are no longer going to be a little "pussy cat" — you are going to grow up and be a lion. Instead of being a little kindly dove — you are going to be a soaring eagle for God. The Church must come to understand that God is calling it to assume its position of authority. The excuses of not being ready, or not being old enough in the Lord, or not having gone to Bible school are no longer acceptable.

God is saying to His Body, "I'm going to bring You into the image of who you really are. I'm going to release you out of the nest. You're going to start acting like kings, and start breathing the life of God into you."

You don't have to accept the concept of defeat while living here on this earth, since man's crown through redemption in Christ is the same as Adam's original crown — GLORY AND HONOR.

When Moses was up in the mountain with God for forty days and nights, God was showing him things. That is how Moses became the author of the Pentateuch (the first five books of the Bible). God lifted up the curtain of revelation to Moses, just as He did to David, and Moses was shown the way man really was created. He waited before God and our God unveiled Genesis 1:26: . . . **Let us make man in our image, after our likeness: and let them have dominion . . . .**

The world view of man is:

"Once I was a tadpole, small and thin;

Then I was a frog with my tail tucked in;

Then I was a monkey in a coconut tree;

Now I am a doctor with a Ph.D."

The born-again child of God refutes the theory of evolution and believes we are created in the image and likeness of God. We as believers picture God's image as nose, eyes, ears, face, legs, arms, hands, etc. We immediately think of the physical attributes of a person, which is only part of the picture of what God is showing us. It is true that we look like God, since the Word does state in Isaiah 59:1, **Behold, the Lord's hand is not shortened, that it cannot save; neither is his ear heavy, that it cannot hear,** and in 2 Chronicles 16:9, **For the eyes of the Lord run to and fro throughout the whole earth . . . .**

It is therefore safe to assume that God does not look like a robot or a creature from outer space, but that He has features just like us, or better yet — that we have features just like Him. We are going to see, however, that God has more in mind than physical attributes.

The image referred to has to do with "after our likeness" and "let them have dominion." The first thing that came out of God's mouth was, "I created man because I want him to assume a place of authority on the earth." There is no truth to the story that God created man because God was "lonely." If God could be lonely, He couldn't be God. Loneliness is an imperfection of the HUMAN personality. When you are lonely, you are sad and depressed. God is a perfect God; therefore, He cannot be lonely, sad or depressed. In fact, God cannot be anything other than PERFECT. He cannot change with situations. (Mal. 3:6, Heb. 13:8.)

The reason for creation is clearly stated in Genesis 1:1,2:

> **In the beginning God created the heaven and the earth.**
>
> **And the earth was without form, and void; and darkness was upon the face of the deep . . . .**

There are three situations here that violate the principles of the character of God:

1. God is not without form.
2. God is not (void) empty.
3. God is not darkness.

There appears to be an alien intruder here, and we clearly see that he did not come after Adam and Eve were placed in the garden. This alien intruder was already here. Therefore, God placed Adam in the garden in order to take his rightful place and have dominion, which is the power and right to govern and control.

> **And God blessed them, and God said unto them, Be fruitful, and multiply, and replenish the earth, and subdue it: and have dominion over the fish of the sea,**

and over the fowl of the air, and over every living thing
that moveth upon the earth.

Genesis 12:8

Why would God use these military terms, **subdue**
or **have dominion** (the right and power to govern and
control), if the Garden of Eden is a place of absolute
perfection? Also note the word **replenish**. The prefix
re affixed to a verb indicates that the action is repeated
or done over, as in *re*-do (do again). Unbeknown to
many Bible readers, Adam was literally commissioned
to "re-do" the earth HIMSELF with the power and
ability given to him by God.

We must understand that it is not the flowers, the
birds, the trees or the atmosphere that makes the
garden good. It is the MAN — placed and commissioned by God with authority to rule — that is keeping the order, keeping the lion and the lamb side by
side, and the serpent under his feet. It is the MAN with
authority who is judging and ruling.

The Bible goes on to state in Genesis 2:15: **And the
Lord God took the man, and put him into the garden
of Eden to dress it and to keep it.** The word *keep* means
to guard, protect and defend. The question is: guard,
protect and defend against what? It must be that there
is an enemy. And that enemy is Satan, as we read
elsewhere in the Word of God.

In Isaiah 14:12 we find a very interesting account:
**How art thou fallen from heaven, O Lucifer, son of
the morning! how art thou cut down to the ground,
which didst weaken the nations!** Also when we refer
to Jesus' words in Luke 10:18, we uncover further proof
of chaos in the beginning. Jesus said, . . . **I beheld Satan
as lightning fall from heaven.**

Please note, Lucifer was evicted from heaven because of his pride. (Is. 14:13,14.) The Bible further states that he was cut down to the ground. We know that here on this planet, the surface is called ground, so Satan (falling from heaven as quickly and as fast as the speed of light), landed on this earth.

And notice, he weakened the nations. He must certainly be responsible for destroying the original creation of the earth. (Thus, Gen. 1:2.) No wonder God places a man called Adam in the Garden of Eden and instructs him to be on guard, to defend, conquer and subdue. It is because there is an enemy of God there, a destroyer, a thief, an alien, who has subverted God's plan — none other than Satan himself, man's life-long enemy.

Additionally, God provides a helper of the same kind, since in His wisdom, He knows that one can chase a thousand, but two can put ten thousand to flight. (Deut. 32:30.)

It is apparent that God meant for Adam to be the god of this world and not Satan. (2 Cor. 4:4.) Satan is only god of this planet because he is sitting in a position that does not belong to him. We will discuss this later on.

God goes on to tell Adam that he has the authority, the power, and the right to govern and control, along with the wisdom, ability and strength. Here is a man who walks through the garden naming 500,000 species of animals, plants, and birds because he is linked up to God with no walls between them. There is nothing hindering Adam from operating in the wisdom of God because the seed of God is in him. He has no problem talking to God in the cool of the day. The best part is, because Adam is operating in his dominion, authority and power, God has no problem talking to him.

Moses too had authority given him by God, and we see him operating in the understanding of this authority when he went before God to plead for the children of Israel, only to be told to use his rod. He could lift his arms and part the Red Sea, and strike the rock for water, because he knew the rod had miracles in it, and he knew who he was. Moses was reminded that he was not ordained by man, but he was ordained by God. (Ex. 3:14.)

He was told to march into Pharaoh's court and tell them, "The Lord God said . . . ." Moses' understanding of his authority enabled him to go. Because Moses knew his authority, God could lift the curtain of revelation and show him that he was operating in the same sphere that God created Adam in.

Notice, again, that man was told to replenish the earth — God did not say He would do it. Likewise, although we know that Jesus is the healer, Jesus is sitting at the right hand of the Father. Therefore, we cannot ask Jesus to come and heal. In Matthew 18:18 He says that the power of binding and loosing is on earth. He even gave His disciples power and authority to cure diseases. (Luke 9:1.)

Remember, the Holy Ghost, sent by the Father after Jesus went to heaven, has come to take Jesus' place on this earth, and He is in you. If He is in you, then He has anointed you the same way Jesus was anointed on this earth. In Acts 10:38 we are reminded:

How God anointed Jesus of Nazareth with the Holy Ghost and with power: who went about doing

good, and healing all that were oppressed of the devil; for God was with him.

The point we need to understand is, Jesus operated on this earth through the anointing of the Holy Spirit, as we must do also. (1 John 2:20, 21:27.) For years the Church has walked down a dark corridor not knowing where it was going, not having any goals, understanding or vision, just wandering and praying, "Oh God, somehow, someway." If we are to get back to God's original plan, we've got to start taking back some of the things in the earth that are ours and belong to us. The Church is beginning to do just that, praise God!

You have to have more than mere head knowledge of God's Word!

We are to have dominion over the works of God's hands. How many times have you allowed the earth to have dominion over you? Fear, bondage, oppression, disease and poverty are all things of this earth. Behind all these lies our biggest enemy, the devil. Christians have crowned him with entirely too much glory because of their fear of him. They have watched him strip finances, destroy health, rob children, break up marriages — and have stood pathetically by, feeling powerless and unable to stop him — UNTIL NOW.

As the Church is taught that God has crowned man with glory and honor from the beginning, and even though Adam lost it, Jesus Christ has regained it for us (1 Cor. 15:22), and has made him to have dominion over all the works of His hands, not just a few, but ALL, and according to Ephesians 1:22, . . . **hath put all things under his feet . . . .** — strength is beginning to well up in the believers.

As God did for David in opening his spiritual eyes to show him man living far below the privileges given him, the Holy Spirit is doing the same today within the Church. Believers are learning to let God's insight, illumination and revelation become personal in their lives.

Unlike David, living under the benefits of the law, we under the better covenant according to Hebrews 8:6, have better promises because the Mediator of our covenant was not a man like Moses — He was Jesus.

God's benevolence and goodness toward those in the Old Testament is the same toward you. The provision of the blessing for us was made in the New Testament in Jesus, and not by observing God's Word through the keeping of the law. In the Old Testament, they received the promises by keeping the law, since they didn't have the inner witness of the Holy Spirit living in them.

In Jeremiah 31:33, God said of His people: . . . I **will put my law in their inward parts, and write it in their hearts** . . . . We now serve God from the law of love that is within us. We no longer have legal obligations, but moral ones from the Holy Spirit, since we are born again by the Holy Spirit, and have the life of God in us. (Refer to John 3:3, 14:17, 1 Cor. 6:17, 2 Cor. 5:17, 1 John 2:20.)

The Position of the Believer

In the first chapter of Ephesians, we are shown that it is through Jesus Christ that we are now born again, filled with the Spirit of God, and come to know the power of God. As a matter of fact, there are over thirty times in the epistles of Paul (Ephesians, Philippians, Colossians, 1 and 2 Timothy, 1 and 2 Thessalonians) that you will read the words "in him," "by him," "of him," "by whom," and "of whom." We are not only physically related to God because we are His creation, but we are spiritually related to Him as His spiritual creation too. We are not next to Him, not near Him, not alongside Him, but IN HIM. . . . **he that is joined unto the Lord is one spirit** (1 Cor. 6:17).

In Ephesians 1:3 Paul goes on to say, **Blessed be the God and Father of our Lord Jesus Christ, who hath blessed us with all spiritual blessings in heavenly places in Christ.** The word **us** here refers to the believer, not every person born in the world. In verse 20 of this chapter Paul makes reference to that **which he** (God) **wrought in Christ, when he raised him from the dead, and set him at his own right hand in the heavenly places.**

When Jesus was raised from the dead, He was set at the right hand of the Father in heaven. If we are raised up with Him, and He is seated at the Father's right hand in heavenly places, then we are seated in heavenly places with Him.

In the Bible, the right hand signifies AUTHORITY. Remember what David said of man in Psalm 8:6, **Thou madest him to have dominion over the works of thy hands . . . .** Words denote specific ideas, and according to Webster's dictionary, *dominion* means supreme authority. Thus this verse indicates that God gave man dominion and authority over His creation.

In Matthew 28:18, Jesus spoke to His disciples AFTER HE WAS RAISED FROM THE DEAD, saying, **. . . All power is given unto me in heaven and in earth.**

The Greek word translated **power** in this verse is *exousia*, meaning authority. When our Lord speaks of heaven, He is referring to the heavenlies because that is the place of principalities, powers and spiritual wickedness in high places. (Eph. 6:12.) What Jesus was saying was that He had the power and authority over demon spirits which traverse the atmosphere. After He was raised from the dead, He could boldly tell His disciples that the power was legally His. Why legally? Because He came into this world the same way every human comes in.

In Galatians 4:4, Paul tells us, **But when the fulness of the time was come, God sent forth his Son, made of a woman, made under the law,** changing the whole picture of the human race. No more types and shadows, fires, tents, clouds, smoke and rods. The stench of the religious tradition of the Pharisees and scribes had come up before God — and He had enough.

A light begins to shine because God is going to invade the human race. Not with an animal or another person, but with HIS SON. This Son would have to be virgin born — eliminating the possibility of His being merely Adam's descendant through Joseph and Mary (or Mary and someone else). If He had sinned, He would also have been disqualified from challenging Satan in the Court of Eternal Justice.

A man had to be found who was authentically human, but unquestionably divine (100% human — 100% divine), in order to become the legally recognized plaintiff.

So Jesus came as an authentic member of the human race. Since He was conceived by the Holy Spirit

24

and virgin born, He was not subject to Satan. The devil could have no legal claim upon Him. In order to establish a legal basis for authority over Jesus, it remained for Satan to ATTEMPT to induce some moral flaw or imperfection of His character or conduct. There was only one way to do this: Satan had to persuade or compel Jesus to break fellowship or unity with His Father, or to pressure Him into rebelling and acting independently. This was Satan's strategy and master plan. This was the crux of the struggle between Jesus and the arch enemy of God and all his forces of darkness, as had been the case in the garden with Adam.

> And the devil said unto him, All this power will I give thee, and the glory of them: for that is delivered unto me; and to whomsoever I will give it.
>
> If thou therefore wilt worship me, all shall be thine.

> Luke 4:6,7

Jesus, being tempted by the devil and using the Word of God to respond, was being taunted with "glory." Notice that the devil didn't say he had stolen the glory, but instead that it had been "delivered" to him. He didn't knock Adam out or steal the glory from him, as some are teaching today. Jesus never challenged Satan's claim to power. He knew that Satan had a legal basis for his claim. He also knew the only way He could redeem and recover man's lost estate was by Calvary — and Jesus told the devil, . . . **Get thee behind me, Satan** . . . . (v. 8). He went on to say to him, . . . **for it is written, Thou shalt worship the Lord thy God, and him only shalt thou serve.**

In other words, Jesus was saying to the devil, "You've got the tables turned, guy. I'm not going to serve you; you're going to serve Me." Jesus knew Who He was serving and the authority He had.

The manger birth was important, but it is overshadowed by the importance of the gory scene of Calvary. The purpose for Jesus' coming was not only to cleanse lepers, cast out devils, heal the sick, and perform miracles. He did not come only to walk on the water and divide the loaves and fishes. He exercised authority over EVERYTHING: nature, demons, sickness, people and religious tradition. The crux of this history of Jesus and the Church is, Calvary — the old rugged cross. CALVARY CONQUERED IT ALL!

History should really be called HIS STORY, because all of the account of man on this planet focuses around that place in Jerusalem, Golgotha — the place of the skull. In John 19:30, when Jesus said, "It is finished," He was not saying, "I am finished," but rather He was stating that the work of restoration was done; redemption was complete. PRAISE GOD! Man would once again be able to be reconciled to God, and God could once again complete His plan.

God's Purpose for Man

The Bible, in 2 Corinthians 6:14, calls the believer "righteousness." It also goes on to call the believer "light" and "the temple of the living God." (v. 16.) Specifically, in Jeremiah and Ezekiel, God says that He will dwell in the believers, walk in them, and be their God.

As a believer who is righteousness and light, and as one acting in the same position as Jesus when He was on this earth, you can approach with confidence, power and authority those who are being held captive by the devil.

The authority, power, and dominion given to Adam was his as long as he retained it. It was by sin that he surrendered that authority. The same is true of you the believer. God takes pleasure when His Body — the Church — starts laying hands on the sick and casting out devils, because we are simply fulfilling His original plan for the human race.

God has never altered His plan. He has never changed His mind or His intentions since He placed Adam in that garden to subdue, conquer, guard, defend, protect, and take dominion over the intruder. God had to supply through another man, Jesus, the person to re-establish the glorious covenant. Not a mere man, not a fallen man, not a man tainted with the blood of fallen man, but a man conceived in the womb of Mary, by the Holy Ghost.

In Galatians 4:1-3, the Bible states that even though you are an heir, if you are a minor child, you cannot inherit the full promises of heirship. Likewise, if you are walking in an immature spiritual state, and your mind is not renewed to the promises of God, even though you are born to be an heir, you are still walking as a slave and a servant. It is a pity to love God, to be saved, to speak in tongues, and yet never grow up into the glorious relationship we have in the Lord Jesus Christ because of an unrenewed, immature mind.

Redeemed man has that same power and authority over the devil because, as it was with Adam, the devil

27

is no match for the born-again, Spirit-filled man. As long as Adam maintained his obedience to God, he walked in total authority, dominion and power in the garden. It was at the point of disobedience that he lost that authority and was then subverted by the attacks of Satan.

Similarly, today's unredeemed man is no match for the devil, and is so easily taken by Satan as he will. (2 Tim. 2:26.) He has no power to resist the devil because he is not controlled by the Spirit of God but is oft times controlled by another spirit. (Eph. 2:2.)

The fourth chapter of Galatians goes on to say that God Himself could not have arbitrarily or lawfully stepped in and repossessed what Adam had given away. Omnipotence undoubtedly had the power to void every attempt of the devil over Adam, but God is a legal and just God. He could not allow Himself to operate simply out of the heritage of His omnipotence. He did it legally, by the birth of a human Son. To the human mind the situation was hopeless. But God found a way.

> But when the fulness of the time was come, God sent forth his Son, made of a woman, made under the law,
>
> To redeem them that were under the law, that we might receive the adoption of sons.
>
> Galatians 4:4,5

We who had been alienated and lost from God were redeemed and reconcilied to Him through His Son. All the destiny of the world and the human race hung on the outcome of the struggle between Jesus and Satan. If Satan could, by any means at his command, have prevailed upon Jesus to have just one thought out of harmony with the Father, he could have resumed

28

his undisputed rule and have become "champ." If he could have seduced the One Whom 1 Corinthians 15:45 calls "the last Adam," as he had done the first Adam, Satan's rulership over the world and mankind would have been forever secure.

But the Bible states in 1 Corinthians 15:21, **For since by man came death, by man came also the resurrection of the dead.**

Ever since that crown was placed on Satan's head in the garden, there had to be much pondering in hell world. Since he too knew the mandate, Satan watched and waited throughout the pages of the Old Testament, for One Who would come through the womb of a human being, never marred by the blood of man. He watched as covenant men were raised up by God, acted like the man in the garden, died and passed the baton onto the next one. He could, undoubtedly, remember his days in the garden, when crawling, sometimes uprightly, he saw and heard the voice of the covenant man Adam. He watched when the covenant man Abraham came along. He saw great men like Moses and the prophets of miracles, Elijah and Elisha, as well as that man after God's own heart, David.

But God was raising up a godly seed of heritage from the fine blood line of Abraham. It was happening because God had made the mandate from Genesis 3:15 that there would be a serpent crusher Who would arise. He came through the most inconspicuous people, even Rahab, a harlot from Jericho whose name appears in the genealogy of Jesus. (Matt. 1:5.) Likewise, David, a man after God's own heart, was shown with all his failures; because all these people were going to foreshadow something and Someone Who was to

29

come. Someone Who had no skeletons hanging in His closet, no marks on His past life, no voices to accuse Him or fingers to point at Him for something He had done. God was making it clear to all mankind that He is not concerned with where you come from and what you did. As long as you are what He says you are now, you can fit into His program.

Yes, the devil watched, knowing that God's man was going to come out of the royal seed. He remembered that covenant promise that God had made to Abraham when He said, "I'm going to cause your children to be like the stars of the sky in number. Out of you I'll bring forth a royal seed, a promised seed." And history is intertwined with the glorious thread of that royal line, of the blood line of Jesus Christ.

Suddenly, in the fullness of time, God sends forth His Son. A new star is in the sky that has never appeared before, and there is a heavenly choir of angels heralding the newborn King. He comes forth in a bizarre way — born in a manger — in a smelly stable, in Bethlehem, of all places.

It was going to be from Bethlehem to Calvary that the conflict would rage. In the effort to recover the lost inheritance of the first Adam, the last Adam and the fallen son of the morning were locked in mortal combat. Through 33 years the struggle continued in undiminished fury.

This fallen Lucifer, once the light bearer and the guardian of the throne of God, the highest of all pre-Adamic created beings, marshalled all the available resources of the underworld in an effort to break down the allegiance of the God-man. That foul fiend, that perverted prince of darkness, did his utmost during the temptation of Jesus in the wilderness, in the opposition of the scribes and Pharisees to His ministry, and even in the garden of Gethsemane, causing Jesus, in a fleeting moment of time to say, . . . **Father, if thou be willing, remove this cup from me** . . . (Luke 22:42), then quickly recovering and adding, . . . **nevertheless, not my will, but thine, be done.**

It was not the prospect of physical suffering that brought the agony in the garden. It was the anguish of a pure soul Who knew no sin, facing the injustice of being made sin for us, as seen in 2 Corinthians 5:21. Of being so completely identified with sin and man's fallen state, not only to forget fellowship with the Father, but becoming the object of the Father's loathing.

Finally, in Pilate's judgment hall and in the crisis of Calvary, the stage was set to force a breakdown in Jesus' allegiance to His Father. Then in Matthew 26:38, He says, . . . **My soul is exceeding sorrowful, even unto death** . . . . With His tortured face streaming with blood drops oozing and splattering to the ground, His mind staggering, His heart breaking under the strain of man's sin and corruption, human language is bankrupt in its attempt to describe the scene around Him.

So gory was the sight that even His disciples walked away. Even though He was God and could have called a multitude of angels to wipe out His enemies in an instant of time, having done so would have meant His suffering was only as a mere man, and His vicarious death would have been nothing more than this gory scene in the annals of history. This was no mere legal impartation of sin, HE WAS MADE SIN. He became the very essence of sin by dying as a sin offering. Since Satan's great purpose in all that he did was to produce in the Son one small thought of rebellion against the Father, when Jesus died without yielding to that pressure, HE CONQUERED! Although He died in doing so, He never questioned the Father. He never pointed an accusing finger saying, "Why Me?"

The devil has attempted, ever since, to cause us to mistrust God and to bring twinges of doubt that come up from the heart, leading the believer to think that God has vacated His throne. When the results of Calvary are appraised, it will appear for what it is, THE TRIUMPH OF THE AGES. When Jesus died without failing in the smallest detail, His death not only resulted in defeating Satan's purpose to obtain a claim upon Him, but it also cancelled every one of Satan's legal claims upon the earth and upon the entire human race, as seen in Hebrews 2:14:

> **Forasmuch then as the children are partakers of flesh and blood, he also himself likewise took part of the same; that through death he might destroy him that had the power of death, that is, the devil.**

A recent translation renders this past phrase, ". . . render to zero him that had power of death, that is the devil."

Satan is not annihilated; however, he is paralyzed. We are not redeemed from the presence of sin; we are redeemed from the power of sin. We are not redeemed from the presence of sicknesss; we are redeemed from the power of sickness. In Romans 6:14 the Apostle Paul tells us: **For sin shall not have dominion over you** . . . . Long before He was put in the grave, the spotless Lamb defeated and destroyed Satan and the power of sin.

Hell was only the final detail of a series of victories that began in the garden of Gethsemane when Jesus said, "I will," and was finalized at the cross saying, "He did." It was an indication of what took place — the keys literally taken out of Satan's hands and the domain of hell broken wide open as the people and saints of God were released from the prisons of darkness. In order to defeat the devil in his own territory, this authentic man with a body, soul and spirit had to descend to hell as seen in Ephesians 4:9: . . . **but that he also descended first into the lower parts of the earth.** The Bible says that He stripped the devil and made a show of him and his demons openly. (Col. 2:15.)

When you were born again, you took upon yourself the nature of Jesus Himself. You now stand before God washed, cleansed, redeemed, sanctified — in other words, just as if you'd never sinned. In 1 Corinthians 15:21,22 Paul states:

> **For since by man came death, by man came also the resurrection of the dead.**

> **For as in Adam all die, even so in Christ shall all be made alive.**

You need to finally understand that God placed back on YOUR head that crown that Adam had placed on Satan's head. Therefore you are not just a pilgrim passing through this earth. Abraham considered himself a pilgrim and a stranger, because he was looking for a city whose builder and maker was God. He was living on a promissory note. We are not strangers or pilgrims, but are here to re-establish the Kingdom of God on this planet.

This world does not belong to the devil! Because of the unrenewed minds of Christians, he has gotten away with all that he is doing. No one has stood up to him and told him to get out.

Christians need to come to the place of the re-established perfect man, as Adam was in this earth, and go back to the same principles of the garden-type living which Adam enjoyed.

We need to see that what God did in Adam, He's also done in us. We need to stop waiting to get to heaven, so we don't have to face the situations that are here on this earth. In John 14:2 Jesus told His disciples, **. . . I go to prepare a place for you.** If we believe that, then we have to believe that it is already done, so there is nothing to worry about as far as heaven is concerned. The real situation to deal with is here. The question is, what are we going to do in the here and now, not in the sweet by and by.

In Romans 3:23, we read, **For all have sinned, and come short of the glory of God;** we see that every man has come short of the position of the glory of God. Every man is born under the Adamic curse, born with the fallen nature of Adam.

As a result of the original sin, every man on earth is born into spiritual death, and has, by nature, inherited that spiritual death. Just like Adam after the fall, every man is living in a state in which he is no longer wearing the crown of God's glory.

It is interesting to note that when Satan tempted Jesus in the wilderness (Luke 4:6), he told Him that he would give Him all the kingdoms of this world (which, by the way, was a lie, since Satan's number one problem is pride; therefore he could not have shared his "glory" with anybody else.) Notice then, that the glory which Adam originally had was delivered into Satan's hand. Satan did not steal it, as has been commonly stated. Rather, it was handed over to him.

Adam was created to live forever. In fact, many scientists agree that the human body was created by God to live forever. In Genesis 2:17, God told Adam not to eat of the tree of the knowledge of good and evil, warning him, . . . **for in the day that thou eatest thereof thou shalt surely die.** Or, as the Hebrew states, "in dying thou shalt surely die." In other words, "dying spiritually, you will die physically."

This is the reason the body wears out and dies. It is through sin that mortality came. We know that even though the body will be placed in the grave and will decay, it is through redemption that our corruptible body is going to be raised an incorruptible body, a body that is shaped after the very body of Jesus when He was raised from the dead. (Rev. 1:5.) It will be an eternal body and will live with God in heaven forever, never decaying, never growing old or dying.

God never designed man to be dominated or controlled by anything or anybody on the face of this earth. Anything that supplants, or takes the place of, your total confidence and trust in the integrity of God is an area of your life that you are being dominated by. It can take the form of fear, or lack, or it can be finances, or it can be sickness. It can be a husband or wife, or it can be children. In other words, ANYTHING that dominates your mind and causes you to think incoherent thoughts concerning something that ought to be right and clear in your thinking is an area of Satan's domination in your life. If there is one way or one place in our life that Satan is stronger than we are, then he is stronger than we are in all of them.

The first chapter of the Gospel of John tells us that when we were born again, God gave us dominion and power to become the sons of God. It is a privilege and honor to become a son of God. Do you realize that when you linked up with God, whether you were rich or poor, educated or not, you became a member of the ROYAL family of God? That means that you changed citizenships. You are no longer a citizen of this world. You changed Lords and tapped into the vast resources of God's glory. You are a son or a daughter of God, born of God, an heir of God; you have received all the fullness God has to offer, and are seated in heavenly places in Christ Jesus.

You were also given the ability to walk in victory. Why would you have to walk in victory if there was nothing to defeat?

As a child of God, you've got a rival, an enemy, who is seeking to destroy you. But amazingly, before you even go into battle, you already know who is going to be the winner! God ALWAYS causes you to triumph. Jesus is your victory!

The Faithfulness of God

Know ye not that the unrighteous shall not inherit the kingdom of God? Be not deceived: neither fornicators, nor idolaters, nor adulterers, nor effeminate, nor abusers of themselves with mankind,

Nor thieves, nor covetous, nor drunkards, nor revilers, nor extortioners, shall inherit the kingdom of God.

1 Corinthians 6:9,10

In verse 11 Paul goes on to remind us that at one time some of us did some of these things before we came to know the Lord and were born again. Yet God shows us in that verse that He doesn't hold anything over our heads. He says that we are **washed,** we are **sanctified**, we are **justified.** The only scars left on us are the scars on our memory; there are no scars in the Book of Life. As far as God is concerned, whatever you and I did before we were born again IS FORGOTTEN.

When we became members of the Kingdom of God and were washed in the blood of Jesus, we were cleansed and washed. All of our sins were taken away. In Psalm 103:12, the psalmist states of God, **As far as the east is from the west, so far hath he removed our transgressions from us.**

You know the story of what Satan did in the garden. In Genesis 3:5, we read that he told Eve about the forbidden tree, **For God doth know that in the day ye eat thereof, then your eyes shall be opened, and ye shall be as gods, knowing good and evil.** He told a half-truth, perverted as it was. Adam and Eve were already gods.

Yes, their eyes were going to be opened, but not in the way Satan so subtly alluded to — that is, in a way to provide spiritual insight — but rather in a way that they would see carnal and natural things they had never seen before.

Adam and Eve already saw spiritual things. Because they walked and communed with God, they didn't have a problem walking by faith and not by sight. In fact, their thoughts were not even plagued with doubt. Faith was in them because the seed of God was in them. Their eyes were opened all right, because of the way they were created. But their eyes would now be opened to see things in reverse. Instead of seeing things through the eyes of God, they would now see things through the eyes of the carnal, fallen nature. They would see things the way many Christians are still seeing things today. They would begin to be moved by circumstances and be led by their senses.

The statement "seeing is believing" must be changed in the Christian's life to "believing is seeing." You'll find out that every time the devil seems to entice people, he says the same old junk. He did it to Jesus also. In Matthew 4:9, he took Him upon a high mountain, **And saith unto him, All these things will I give thee, if thou wilt fall down and worship me.** Satan untimately wants to receive worship. He has always had a great "ego problem." Everything he does is geared to eventually getting the upper hand on us.

This is a good lesson to learn; each time you seem to be motivated by "ego" or "pride," recognize where it comes from and, in the Name of Jesus, cast it down!

Fear, the Perverted Force of Satan

When Adam and Eve fell in the garden, the first thing they realized was that they were naked. For the first time they saw their nakedness and experienced fear. In Genesis 3:10, the first thing that Adam said to God (after God had pursued and found him) was, **. . . I heard thy voice in the garden, and I was afraid . . . .** The first thing sown into a spirit dead to God (or separated from God) is the perverted force of fear, and that fear will produce like faith.

Fear will produce the perverted results of Satan's attempts to destroy you and your life — if you allow it to. As faith is the force of God, fear is the force of Satan.

Some may ask, "How does fear produce?" All you have to do is think of your own life. Can you recall times in your life when you imagined things that you had no basis for, and it seemed that some of those things actually came to pass in your life?

Think of the life of Job. In Job 3:25, after catastrophe had come upon him, he said, **For the thing which I greatly feared is come upon me, and that which I was afraid of is come unto me.**

What was it that Job feared? Catastrophe, loss of riches, loss of cattle, etc. These pictures of loss and tragedy were already in Job's mind, and actually contributed to what happened to him. Some people argue vehemently against this concept, saying, "What will be, will be." They believe we have no control over our lives. I want you to notice what is said of God in Hebrews 2:15 in *The Amplified Bible:*

> **And also that He might deliver and completely set free all those who through the (haunting) fear of death, were held in bondage throughout the whole course of their lives.**

In Romans 8:15, Paul tells us, **For ye have not received the spirit of bondage again to fear . . . .** One of the great privileges of the New Birth is victory over fear. I believe we can see by this verse that God, the Father of the new creation, sees the perverted power of fear and assures the believer at the New Birth that freedom from fear is one of his first great privileges.

> The fear of man brings a snare, but whoever leans
> on, trusts and puts his confidence in the Lord is safe
> and set on high.

Proverbs 29:25 AMP

Notice, Adam said to God, "And I heard thy voice in the garden." Even when you are spiritually dead, you still hear the voice of God. You may not want to listen because you know in your state of spiritual death (Eph. 2:1,2), that if you listen to His voice you have got to change. A nonbeliever does not hear God's voice when it comes to revelation knowledge or illumination, but he does hear God's voice saying, "Repent, change, better not do that."

Some Christian might come along with a tract and say, "Jesus loves you," or someone might be standing on a soap box saying, "Repent, the Kingdom of God is at hand." As the unbeliever walks by, he might think to himself, "Oh, that guy is crazy." But when he is laying his head on his pillow, he may ponder the possibility of that "crazy guy" being right.

Even to the fallen state of humanity, God is speaking. God commands all men, everywhere, to repent. In 1 Timothy 2:4, the Apostle Paul speaks of God, **Who will have all men to be saved, and to come to the knowledge of the truth.** God's Word also states in Titus 2:11, **For the grace of God that bringeth salvation hath appeared to all men.** This chapter goes on to say in verse 12, **Teaching us that, denying ungodliness and worldly lusts . . . .**

This shows that grace appears to everybody, to call them to salvation. But notice, it states that it is the believer (each of us) who is taught. Why? Because the believer is in fellowship with God. The unbeliever is separated from God; therefore he is only going to do what comes naturally, that is, to sin. The believer is going to be taught to deny all that is in the world, because, by the Spirit of God living in him, he knows sin separates him from God. Therefore, he will do all he can to walk not only in relationship with God but also in fellowship with Him.

Where's the Glory?

In Psalm 78:60, the psalmist, recounting Israel's plight throughout the wilderness up to the Promised Land, says of God, **So that he forsook the tabernacle of Shiloh, the tent which he placed among men.** Shiloh was the appointed place of the tabernacle, but the keepers of the tent in Shiloh, the Ephraimites, had become loose in their living.

God said, "I'm not going to honor a place where people do not honor Me, and I'm not going to bless a people who do not honor Me." The verse says that He "forsook the tabernacle" — He left, moved out.

The same God Who had instructed the Israelites to construct the tabernacle so He could be among them, now says, "I will no longer be there with you, because of your disregard for Me."

In verse 61, the psalmist goes on to say, **And delivered his strength into captivity, and his glory into the enemy's hand,** referring to Israel's strength and glory, not God's glory.

No one can take away God's glory, as we see in Malachi 3:6 in which He states, **For I am the Lord, I**

41

change not . . . . And in Hebrews 13:8 we read, **Jesus Christ the same yesterday, and to day, and for ever.** God had given His glory to the Israelites in the Ark. It was their secret weapon. With the glory of God with them, they were invincible. The enemy had no chance. Without God's glory, they were helpless.

Again notice, as with Adam, it was not that God was removing Himself, it was that man was contributing to his own demise. Someone has artfully said, "If there is a gap between you and God, then somebody moved, and it was NOT God." The only way to maintain your position of authority with God is to make sure you stay close.

In John 15:5 Jesus said, **I am the vine, ye are the branches: He that abideth in me, and I in him, the same bringeth forth much fruit: for without me ye can do nothing.**

God does not look at things the way man does, nor does He do things the way man does. It was in spite of our walking away from Him that He pursued us and gave us eternal life through His Son Jesus. GOD IS A GOOD GOD.

If you could envision what took place on Golgotha, the person hanging on the middle cross should be you and me. It is, of course, Jesus — Who WILLINGLY went in our place. God provided for man's redemption from the very beginning. Jesus, Who knew no sin, came to earth and was made to be sin for us, that we might be made the righteousness of God in Him. You now, in Christ, have everything you need to be what God has called you to be.

Mighty Warriors

The Church is coming into a new dimension in God. We are leaving behind the rags of our religious traditions and the doctrines of men, and are growing up. As seen in Ephesians 4:15, the Church is coming into the measure of the stature of Christ — not the measure of a man.

We're growing up into the Lord Jesus Christ, He is our example. The believers are being challenged in this day for one primary purpose and reason — TO COME TO MATURITY. The Spirit of God is speaking all over the world, "Grow up, Church, and come into the fullness of who you are and realize that you are somebody in God."

God is no longer winking at our ignorance. He used to wink at the ignorance of some of us in days gone by, when we would say, "I think I'm getting sick," or, "I'll never get to the place where I'd like to be." Ignorance, unbelief, and doubt will abort the seed of God from finding its rightful place in your spirit man, and therefore not produce the quality of that seed in your life.

There is a method of birth control used in the world today. It is called an Intra-Uterine Device, better known as an I.U.D. It is a widely used contraceptive that prevents conception when it is planted in the female uterus.

The I.U.D. prevents the seed of the man from uniting with the seed of the woman to produce a baby. Actually, the I.U.D. makes her unfruitful and barren. This so beautifully relates to the believer. The Bible says the seed is the Word of God. (Mark 4:14.) It is to be sown on good ground to produce, according to the parable Jesus taught about the sower. (Mark 4.)

I believe that, more than anything else, it is the reception of the Word of God in our lives that will produce results. In 1 Peter 1:23, the Word of God is called the incorruptible seed. We notice, however, that 2 Peter 1:8 shows that there are some believers who are barren, or who do not produce for God. We can safely say that Satan's method of aborting the birth and growth of the Word is also an I.U.D.: IGNORANCE, UNBELIEF, DOUBT. These are the three major reasons why the seed does not produce. Remember, something that is not conceived can never be born.

Because the presentation of the Word has brought new vitalized life to the Body of Christ, we now see things as we have never seen them before. For example, John 3:3 states, . . . **Except a man be born again, he cannot see the kingdom of God.** I used to think that meant heaven in the sky and the new Jerusalem. I've come to find out that the word **see** in this verse doesn't mean that at all. Instead it means "to perceive and understand." It is only applied to that person who has been regenerated by the power of God. That means the ability to clearly understand the mind, purpose, plan and will of God for our lives. The unbeliever cannot understand this, he is lost. His mind is alienated from God.

In 1 Peter 2:9 the apostle speaks of the Lord . . . **who hath called you out of darkness into his marvellous light.** Here we are shown that there is no way you can remain in spiritual darkness when you are a follower of the Lord Jesus Christ. God commands that light come into you, whether you like it or not.

To all those who have said they cannot understand the Bible, the Lord points out in John 7:17, **If any man will do his will, he shall know of the doctrine . . . .** The word **doctrine** simply means the teachings of the Lord Jesus Christ. Sound doctrine must be restored to the Body of Christ. The Body of Christ must grow up and realize that you don't have to be a graduate of a local college or go across country to a Bible school. All you need to do is to be a believer, since your eyes have already been exposed to the glorious light through the Gospel of Jesus Christ.

Thank God for the academic degrees that hang on our walls, but all they are are pieces of paper. The simple believer who may never have gone to the first grade has the same ability to understand and to know the things of God as the highly educated believer. There is only one thing that will block the entrance of God's Word from bringing light, and that is ignorance remaining in you. The seed of God will produce life.

We are not living in the age of doom. Turn off your T.V. or radio when you hear somebody talking negatively. We are not living in the time of despair and unbelief, we are living in the Church Age. The Bible says it is the age of the Holy Ghost, and the age of the Holy Ghost is an AGE OF POWER (authority).

The Church is not going out a tattered Bride; it is going out a glorious Church without spot or wrinkle. It is going out as a Church that is flowing in the anointing. It is time for the Body of Christ to FUNCTION WITH THE UNCTION. (Joel 2:1-14.)

The time has come for holiness to begin in the house of God. God is saying to the Church, "Get your act together and get your churches in order, because I'm getting ready to move by My Spirit, and you've got to clean out the junk."

Colossians 3:10 states, **And have put on the new man . . . .,** pointing the believer to understand that when he puts on the new man, God has already put something on the inside of him, by the Holy Spirit, called the New Birth. What God puts on the inside, man has to put on outwardly to match. I'm not talking about the length of skirt that ladies wear, I'm talking about the kind of life that is lived as a testimony before the world.

The verse goes on to say, **. . . which is renewed in knowledge after the image of him that created him.** The image of God is one of dominion and authority; the power and right to govern and control with the ability to replenish the earth and subdue it. These are the images God is restoring to His Body so it can grow up to its authority and see itself in the image of God, instead of in the image of failure and frustration.

DO NOT be fooled, we don't have two personalities, one following God and the other following the devil; and we are not merely "redone" on the inside.

> **Therefore if any man be in Christ, he is a new creature: old things are passed away; behold, all things are become new.**
>
> **2 Corinthians 5:17**

The Church CAN NOT do it for you, nor can the preacher tell you how to do it. You CAN NOT ever learn it in a new believer's class. You will learn it by studying the Word of God, putting off what you used to believe, and acting on what you now know by the Word of God. Do not forget, God will allow what you allow. (Matt. 16:19.)

Jesus came to put into man what Satan had taken out. He also came to take out of man what Satan had put in — our attitude and perverted thinking. We must start realizing that we are not who we used to be, and are becoming who we already are in Christ from the New Birth. This means that who we become will be greater than who we are now, because who we are going to be is the image of God's dear Son. Although we have not arrived, we are growing up into the measure of the fullness of the stature of Christ. That measure being — the ability to walk in His same anointing.

> **If there be a messenger with him, an interpreter, one among a thousand, to shew unto man his uprightness:**
>
> **Then he is gracious unto him, and saith, Deliver him from going down to the pit: I have found a ransom.**
>
> Job 33:23,24

This passage indicates a searching for someone to tell man who God really is: the author of good; a loving, sovereign, upright God. Verses 25 through 28 go on to say,

> **His flesh shall be fresher than a child's: he shall return to the days of his youth:**
>
> **He shall pray unto God, and he will be favourable unto him: and he shall see his face with joy: for he will render unto man his righteousness.**
>
> **He looketh upon men, and if any say, I have sinned, and perverted that which was right, and it profited me not;**

**He will deliver his soul from going into the pit,
and his life shall see the light.**

When the "faith" message came along (just one
vehicle used by God), we got that "interpreter," "one
among a thousand" who gave us the word of life and
victory. We found out we did not have to be poor,
miserable, and under the condemnation of sin. We
found out that, for a long time, even the Church of the
Lord Jesus Christ — the glorious Bride — had been
walking in darkness in many areas.

Oh, we were saved, but we were just getting to
heaven because we were "holding on until the end."
It is through the uncompromised Word — the truth of
God — that we learn, and keep on learning, that we
can live the redeemed life on this planet and in this
world, that we can be delivered from going down to
the pit, that we can walk in joy and in the freshness
of our youth, that we can have all the things in God's
Book reaffirmed and re-established in our lives.

It was ignorance that caused us to walk in darkness
and in the shadows of the night, barely touching the
benefits of God's eternal promises to us. Instead of
being in the center of God's divine blessing, we have
watched from the outside and said, "I hope I can be
that way, and someday be there."

God desires to move in the Body of Christ TODAY,
with a move of His Spirit, in a way that we have never
seen before. The last day is the day of the greatest
revival. It is going to come about because the people
of God have walked back to the place where God's
glory can come into the tabernacle — when whole
church services will be turned over to God's power and
presence.

There is a day coming when people are not going to be urged or coerced out of their seats to come and receive Jesus. They are going to fall on their knees and repent with tears, while crawling to the altar to bow before God. This time is being ushered in through praise and through worship. In the last day, there will be a restoration of the tabernacle of David with great praise coming out of the people.

Praise is the key to victory in battle, but it is worship that brings God on the scene. That is what is going to happen as the people of God get caught up and focus their attention on Him, getting their eyes off personalities and things around themselves. There will be a great restoration of God's power to the Church of Jesus Christ. It is not only going to be power coming out of our mouths; it will also come from our actions. It is going to come through our hands and through a great restoration of spiritual gifts to the Body of Christ.

The ministers of the Gospel are going to begin to operate in the revelation gifts. They will stand in the pulpit and know, by the word of knowledge, things that have already taken place in people's lives. By the gift of discerning of spirits, they will be able to recognize, not only demons, but angels all around. They will, by the gift of the word of wisdom, begin to speak, through prophetic utterance, things that are going to come to pass in the days ahead.

All these things will take place because God is returning this supernatural power to the Church again. The blinders are being removed, and God is saying to the Church in this day, "You've already received your place of power and authority when you became a partaker of the divine nature. You are already established in the kingdom of My dear Son. You have already received the kingdom principles in your life — now wake up and realize that there is an interpreter, a messenger, who has come to declare life, freedom and the knowledge of your redemption in the Lord."

We have given the devil too much glory! How could the devil steal from God's under-ruler on the earth? How could he steal from the real god of this world? He couldn't steal anything from Adam because Adam had dominion over HIM (Adam had to deliver that glory to the devil himself — notice Luke 4:6). Satan can't steal anything from us either, other than what we allow him to take. He is the kind of thief who cannot invade our house if we keep him off limits. Praise God, the gates of hell shall not prevail against the Church!

Remember, being tempted is not a sin. If temptation was a sin, Jesus was a sinner, and we know He was not because He did not yield, give in, surrender, or allow Himself to be dominated by the temptation.

Satan, from the very beginning, wanted the power, dominion and authority that had been given to Adam. He knew if that power remained in Adam, he was going to be dominated by man. He also knew that if he could get the power away from Adam, he could dominate man. He would then be able to thwart the plan of God and stop God from using man on this earth.

That is what happened when Adam fell. He literally took the crown of glory that God had placed upon his head and surrendered it to one called Satan. That glory was delivered into the hands of the enemy.

As a believer, you also go through a legitimate wilderness experience when you are born again. You come out of darkness into the marvelous light of God and begin to get your bearings. You don't know where you are going, and sometimes even feel as though you are going to lose everything. You get to the other side of the wilderness, having watched God bless you and having experienced His hand of power upon you. You stand on the brink of the Jordan River. You look over into the Promised Land, seeing the walled cities of Jericho and listening to the voice of the servants of God saying, "We're going over to the other side."

In many, fear rises up, and they say, "Take me back. I want no war, no struggling, and no action. I'm afraid." So, too, the Israelites decided they weren't going God's way. They turned back and had their own wilderness experience.

God said, "If that's what you want, you can have it." According to Numbers 32:13, a whole generation was wiped out; they wandered in that wilderness **. . . until all the generation, that had done evil in the sight of the Lord, was consumed.** It was a thirty-eight-and-one-half-year experience during which time God got rid of all the bickering, murmuring, complaining, and backbiting — all of the sins of the human spirit, not the sins of the flesh.

Through the mouth, we can commit sins of the spirit which are different from the sins of the flesh. A sin of the flesh may offend and hurt you and even bring you out of fellowship with God. A sin of the spirit, such as bickering and backbiting (with your tongue), can affect the whole Body of Christ as an evil cancer.

The devil thought he had won the victory, but here was a new group of people coming down the road. All the backbiters, murmurers and complainers had died in the wilderness. God had raised up a whole new generation under the leadership of Joshua, trained under the ministry of Moses.

Today, a whole new generation of people is again being raised up. The "Word movement" has built up a people tired of the traditions and weights of religion. It is a generation which walks up to the water and says, "Open up." It is a generation which is no longer concerned with anything else except following God. They have seen all the miracles, they have seen all the power, and now they have a new direction because the Word has been put in their mouths and it is the Word that is going to bring them over the Jordan into the Promised Land.

In John 17:4,5 Jesus prayed to the Father in heaven:

> **I have glorified thee on the earth: I have finished the work which thou gavest me to do.**
>
> **And now, O Father, glorify thou me with thine own self with the glory which I had with thee before the world was.**

Notice that Jesus said **had,** which meant that the glory He operated with on the earth was not the glory that He operated with in heaven. While on the earth, He operated with the glory that came by the power and anointing of the Holy Spirit, not as God but as a man filled with God's glory.

In verse 22, Jesus goes on to say of His disciples, **And the glory which thou gavest me I have given them** . . . . Jesus stands on the mount and transfers, by the power of attorney, that glory He operated with on the earth.

> **. . . In my name shall they cast out devils; they shall speak with new tongues;**

52

> They shall take up serpents; and if they drink any
> deadly thing, it shall not hurt them; they shall lay
> hands on the sick, and they shall recover.

Mark 16:17,18

Begin to see Adam as a man set on guard, a man created by God to be firm and strong. See a man taking complete dominion over the whole Garden of Eden. If you can see that — you can see yourself in the same light. Through Jesus, man is no longer defeated or a failure. He is victorious, he governs and is not governed, he controls and is not controlled. He dominates and is not dominated.

As we read in Luke, Chapter 9, Jesus appointed twelve disciples and sent them out. When they were sent forth, they were given power and authority. The power and cure is always Jesus — but He put that power and cure in our hands. That is why He said, "Lay hands on the sick, and they shall recover." Without Him we are nothing, but with Him we can boldly proclaim who we are, because of Who He is, and what He has made us to be.

As with the twelve who were sent forth, look at yourself as the light and righteousness of God. See yourself as sanctified. When you pray, realize that you can get the same results that Jesus did when He prayed. Acknowledge, as Jesus did, that you know the Father hears you when you pray. From this understanding, you obtain the same results.

The next time the devil tries to tell you that the pain in your chest is a heart attack, start saying, "HOLD EVERYTHING. IN THE NAME OF JESUS, I HAVE AUTHORITY OVER YOU AND I COMMAND YOU TO LET GO AND LEAVE ME ALONE!" Continue to say,

"I'M A CHILD OF GOD. I'M LIGHT. I'M RIGHTEOUSNESS. I'M SANCTIFIED. I'M WASHED. I'M CLEANSED. I'M JUSTIFIED." Keep using the NAME of Jesus, because it is the NAME of Jesus that sealed Satan's fate.

In Acts 29, we read about the seven sons of Sceva who tried to do the same miracles that Paul was doing in Ephesus. They thought they could command the devil.

Their failure came about because they had no relationship with God. The names of those seven sons were not written in the Book of Life, and therefore, they had no power, no authority. They could not command anything.

Authority is the result of relationship. Therefore, don't gloat in the power that you have in all this authority. Don't rejoice in that. Rejoice that your name is written in the Lamb's Book of Life and that you have the authority to take your rightful place on this earth as a mighty warrior, victorious in all circumstances.

My desire is that you will begin to walk in the privileges provided by Jesus when He regained man's crown. And that you will allow God's insight, illumination and revelation to rule each day of your life.

Remember, you now stand before God washed, cleansed, redeemed and sanctified. In fact, you have become a member of the Royal Family of God. So hold fast to the truths in the Word of God. Even when the winds of adversity come, start soaring like an eagle!

Know beyond a shadow of a doubt who YOU are in Christ and maintain your position of authority with God, through a close relationship.

Study the Word of God, putting off what you used to believe that did not conform to the Word of God. Begin acting on what you now know by the Word.

Finally, make a decision to know God, because in knowledge there is confidence, and in confidence there is faith, and in faith there is — DOMINION AND AUTHORITY TO RULE AND REIGN.